THE LIBRARY OF AMERICAN LIVES AND TIMES™

SOJOURNER TRUTH

From Slave to Activist for Freedom

Mary G. Butler

The Rosen Publishing Group's
PowerPlus Books™
New York

To Alex, so she can learn more about the life and legacy of "The Lady," Sojourner Truth

Published in 2003 by The Rosen Publishing Group, Inc.
29 East 21st Street, New York, NY 10010

Copyright © 2003 by The Rosen Publishing Group, Inc.

First Edition

Editor's Note: All quotations have been reproduced as they appeared in the letters and diaries from which they were borrowed. No correction was made to the inconsistent spelling that was common in that time period.

Library of Congress Cataloging-in-Publication Data

Butler, Mary G., 1943–
Sojourner Truth : from slave to activist for freedom / Mary G. Butler.
    p. cm. — (The library of American lives and times)
Includes bibliographical references (p.) and index.
  ISBN 0-8239-5736-5 (library binding)
1. Truth, Sojourner, d. 1883—Juvenile literature. 2. African American abolitionists—Biography—Juvenile literature. 3. African American women—Biography—Juvenile literature. 4. Abolitionists—United States—Biography—Juvenile literature. 5. Social reformers—United States—Biography—Juvenile literature. [1. Truth, Sojourner, d. 1883. 2. Abolitionists. 3. Reformers. 4. African Americans—Biography. 5. Women—Biography.] I. Title. II. Series.
  E185.97.T8 B88 2003
  305.5'67'092—dc21

                                                    2001006169

Manufactured in the United States of America

CONTENTS

1. Slavery in America

Sunday school teachers were holding a convention in Battle Creek, Michigan, in June 1863. Several men had already spoken about teaching issues, and the audience was getting restless. Then a voice came from the rear of the hall, asking, "Is there an opportunity now that I might say a few words?" The question created an electric effect in the hall as five hundred people instantly rose to their feet. The famous Sojourner Truth was going to speak!

A tall black woman moved slowly through the crowd to the podium. She turned to the audience and said in a low, rich voice:

> *I want to speak of the great sin of prejudice against color . . . . My children, who made your skin white? Was it not God? Who made mine black? Was it not the same God? Am I to blame,*

Opposite: This is an 1864 photo of Sojourner Truth, one of the most famous African American women of the nineteenth century. A former slave, she gained fame as an abolitionist and a women's rights activist.

therefore, because my skin is black? . . . . Now children, remember what Sojourner Truth has told you, and thus get rid of your prejudice, and learn to love colored children that you may all be the children of your Father who is in Heaven.

Sojourner Truth, who spoke so movingly about the evil of prejudice, was one of the most well known people in America. She was born a slave, but about twenty years after she was freed, she became celebrated around the whole country as a powerful crusader against slavery and all forms of injustice.

When Truth spoke to the Sunday school teachers, America was in the middle of the Civil War (1861–1865). This conflict was largely about whether slavery would continue to exist in the United States. The Southern states, called the Confederacy, wanted to keep slavery. The Northern states, called the Union, wanted to outlaw slavery.

Slavery existed in the Americas long before the United States was first settled. As early as 1585, the English ship *Jesus* brought slaves to Haiti, an island in the Caribbean Sea, south of present-day Florida. Slavery got its start in North America in 1619, when twenty Africans were brought on a Dutch ship to Jamestown, Virginia.

Opposite: This military map of the United States was published by Bacon & Company in 1862. The areas shown in pink and yellow were slave states belonging to the Confederacy around that time. Green areas were free, or nonslaveholding, states.

BACON
MILITARY MAP
UNITED S?
Shewing the
FORTS & FORTIF?

Published by BACON & C?   LONDON.

EXPLANAT?

Free or Non-Slaveholding States.
Population 18,000,000, Area 1,8?

Border Slave States.
Pop.? 3,000,000, 507,000 are Sla?

Seceded or Confederate States
Pop.? 10,000,000, 3,500,000 are Sla?

In the mid-1800s, more than three million African Americans were enslaved in the South. Thousands of slaves attempted to run away to freedom in the North. It was illegal, and dangerous, for a slave to do this. Masters chased the fugitives, often using dogs to track and to capture them. When slaves were caught, they were beaten, sold, or even killed. Slaves who tried to escape had to travel secretly, usually at night. They traveled north toward freedom, using the Underground Railroad. This was neither underground nor an actual railroad. It was an informal network of hiding places where "conductors" offered slaves food and a safe place to sleep. By night the fleeing "passengers" traveled by foot, by wagon, or by boat. They hoped to reach freedom in the northern states, where slavery was no longer legal, or in Canada, where slavery was not allowed. Most of the conductors were white abolitionists. However, there were also many free blacks, as well as former slaves, who helped the runaways to reach freedom.

By the time of the American Revolution (1775–1783), when the colonies won their freedom from Great Britain, slavery existed in every part of British North America. The number of slaves increased the farther south one went from New York to Virginia. By the mid-1800s, the largest slave populations could be found on plantations in the Carolinas, Alabama, Mississippi, and Louisiana. These southern states, where most of the slaves lived and worked, were the most opposed to ending slavery.

Some voices had begun protesting against slavery as early as the mid-1700s. Members of the Society of Friends, known as Quakers, were among the first to say slavery was wrong. They continued to be among the most active opponents of slavery and later were active helping fugitive slaves escape through the Underground Railroad.

At the start of the American Revolution, several hundred thousand slaves lived in the colonies. About three thousand black men fought in the Colonial army, hoping their military service would earn them freedom. Yet after the war, many were sent back to their owners, who then collected the slaves' war pensions.

By 1804, almost all the northern states had abolished slavery. Slavery was still legal in the southern states. Four years later, the federal government made it illegal to bring more slaves from Africa into any state.

Between 1619 and 1808, however, more than 450,000 Africans had been brought to America as

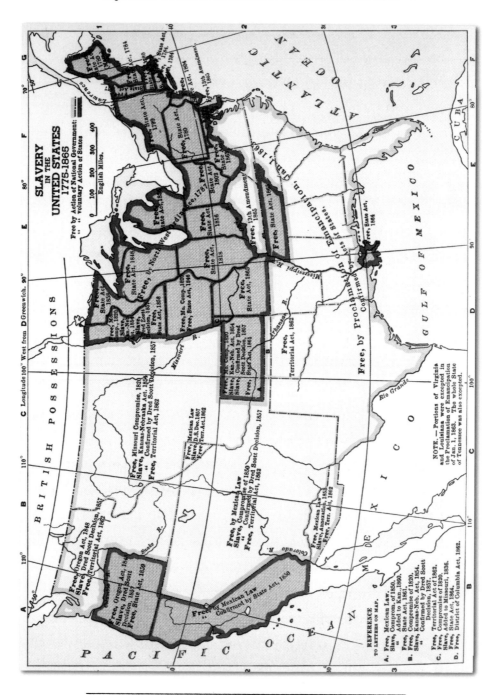

This undated map illustrates the distribution of slavery in the United States between 1785 and 1865.

This hand-colored woodcut shows captured Africans being taken into slavery in the 1700s. Slaves who were caught in the interior of Africa were forced to walk hundreds of miles (km) to get to the coast, where ships waited to take them away. Many slaves died on these marches.

slaves. They were captured in Africa and were packed into ships for the terrible journey across the ocean. This voyage could take from three weeks to three months, depending on the size of the ship and whether there were any storms on the ocean.

Many people died on this voyage because men, women, and children were forced to live in cramped, unhealthy quarters in the lower decks of the ship. They received little food and almost no fresh air or exercise. Disease spread among the captives, because there was no way to keep their quarters clean. On a few ships, most slaves died before they reached America. The average death rate of the captured Africans was about 20 percent.

The auction block awaited the individuals and the

Pictured here is the crowded slave deck of the *Wildfire*, a ship that sailed into Key West, Florida, on April 30, 1860. To maximize profits, slave merchants carried as many slaves as was physically possible on their ships.

families who did survive this ordeal. The cries of parents and children echoed through the auction halls as young ones were torn from their mothers' arms.

In the 1700s, slaves sent to the middle Atlantic or the northern states usually worked on small farms or as household servants. Many lived in cities and learned trades, such as shipbuilding or blacksmithing. In general, the slaves in the northern states were treated better than were the slaves in the South. In the North, living conditions were less harsh. Beatings and other severe punishments were less frequent in the North, and slaves had more opportunities to learn new skills and to better their condition.

In Virginia, slaves usually grew tobacco, raised livestock, or worked on small farms. In the Carolinas and Georgia, slaves grew rice and harvested indigo for dye. Sugarcane plantations were common in the Gulf Coast states, such as Louisiana. Some cotton was grown in the South, but it was not yet the most profitable crop.

This drawing by William L. Sheppard shows slaves using a cotton gin on an American plantation in the 1800s. The gin could clean seeds from 50 pounds (23 kg) of cotton per day.

The whole economic life of the South changed almost overnight in 1793, when Eli Whitney patented the cotton gin. His new invention made it possible for slaves to remove the seeds from the cotton plant ten times faster than they could by hand. At the same time, the textile industry in England was demanding more and more American cotton. The increased export market and more efficient production methods meant that plantation owners needed even more slaves to work in the expanded cotton fields.

For a few years, this tremendous demand for slave

labor in the South was fed by increased shipments of slaves from Africa. After 1808, it was no longer legal to bring slaves from Africa into the United States. This meant that southern plantation owners had to find more slaves from another source. They bought slaves from northern and border states in ever-increasing numbers. By 1860, it is estimated that about four million African Americans were living in the South.

After slaves from northern or border states were sold to a new southern plantation owner, then they were herded into groups for the trip south. The women were tied together with ropes. The men were handcuffed in pairs. The slaves were then chained together in larger groups. They were forced to march from 25 to 30 miles (40–48 km) per day in all kinds of weather, down rutted roads, until they reached their new living quarters.

The majority of these slaves, both men and women, worked in cotton or sugar fields. Conditions were brutal for these field workers. They worked six days per week from sunrise to sunset and were beaten by white overseers for any disobedience. Some of the more fortunate men were employed as skilled artisans or as factory workers. A few slaves, mostly women, worked in the plantation houses as cooks, nannies, or maids.

More than the working conditions, it was the unconditional submission required by slavery that made life intolerable for the blacks. One master described the slaveholders' attitude toward blacks: "We teach them they are slaves . . . and that to the white belongs control and to the black obedience." Slaves had no control over their lives. Their masters controlled all parts of slaves' lives, including where they lived, whom they married, what kind of work they did, and even what they ate.

In some northern states, slaves could learn to read and to write. In the South, it was illegal for any slave to do so. Southern plantation owners feared that if their slaves learned to read, they would learn about human rights. Slaves might learn ways to unite and to free themselves. Slaves were denied the comfort of organized religion, because they were not permitted to gather in groups and their ministers were forbidden to preach.

The slaves became skilled at leading double lives. In public they had to show obedience to their masters. They could keep their self-respect in private, however. One slave explained, "I got one mind for the white folk to see, another for what I know is me." Slaves commonly rebelled against the system in small ways, such as by stealing and by lying. Escape to freedom in the North was the ultimate rebellion.

In the southern states, where the blacks often out-numbered the whites, there was constant fear that slaves would run away or would rebel against their masters. All blacks were required to carry a pass if they left their plantations to do errands for their masters. Slaves who tried to escape were punished severely. They were whipped, mutilated, or branded. The men

> *In U.S. history,*
> *during the three decades*
> *before the Civil War, abolitionists*
> *strove to end slavery. Abolitionists were*
> *members of a movement that aimed first to end*
> *the slave trade and then to abolish the institution*
> *of slavery. The abolitionist movement helped*
> *to free millions of black people from*
> *bondage, as well as to restore*
> *their human rights*
> *and dignity.*

could be punished by being sold to another plantation and by being separated from their families. Some slaves were even executed. Any white person who helped slaves to escape could be punished with fines.

Men and women opposed to slavery were known as abolitionists. The earliest abolitionist groups, founded in the Revolutionary War era, worked to end slavery gradually. Quakers, Methodists, and other religious groups assisted escaping slaves and worked through the legal system to end slavery. They did not want to use violent means to free slaves.

As the southern demand for slaves increased,

opposition to slavery grew in the North. Many abolitionists were no longer content to work slowly through the
courts. These men and women, known as activists, wanted faster ways to free slaves. The activist abolitionist
movement to end slavery was triggered in 1831, when
William Lloyd Garrison published the first issue of his
newspaper, *The Liberator* in Boston, Massachusetts.
Garrison wrote articles supporting the immediate emancipation of slaves, with no financial compensation to owners. Radical, or activist, abolitionists did more than write
articles. They helped runaway slaves escape through the
Underground Railroad. They discussed separating the
northern states from the southern slaveholding states.

The conflict between the North and the South over
slavery worsened in the 1840s and the 1850s. The southern states felt threatened by the activist antislavery atti-
tudes of many people in the North. They felt that their
economic survival depended on the use of slaves.

Finally, in December 1860, the South Carolina legislature voted to separate from the United States. The
Confederate States of America were established and the
Civil War began. This four-year war was the bloodiest in
the nation's history and almost destroyed the country.
When it ended in 1865, however, the nation had survived
the challenge, and slavery was abolished.

Sojourner Truth played an important part in the
movement to end slavery. Yet, her early life gave little
hint of the role she would have later in this struggle.

2. The Slave Isabella

In 1797, George Washington had just ended his second term as U.S. president and had retired to his home at Mount Vernon, Virginia. In or close to that year, a baby was born to Betsey and James, a slave couple living in New York State. This baby was named Isabella. Like her parents, she had no last name, because slaves were only given first names. They sometimes used the last names of their owners. Isabella was the youngest of ten or twelve children. Only Isabella and her older brother Peter still remained with their parents. Almost all of Isabella's brothers and sisters had already been taken from the family and sold. It was common for slave families to be broken up and for children to be sold to other owners. Slaves had no power to prevent this.

One of Isabella's earliest memories was of her mother, known as Mau-Mau Bett, telling stories of her other children being taken from her. Isabella would one day record in her autobiography, the *Narrative of Sojourner Truth*, the following tale about her mother.

Mau-Mau Bett used to point to the stars and tearfully tell Isabella, "Those are the same stars, and that is the same moon, that look down on your brothers and sisters, and which they see as they look up at them, though they are ever so far away from us and from each other."

Isabella and her family were owned by Johannes Hardenbergh, who had a small farm in Ulster County, about 90 miles (145 km) north of New York City. This area near the Hudson River had been settled by Dutch families in the 1600s. Baby Isabella grew up hearing and speaking only Dutch, which was spoken by her master and by her parents.

When Isabella was a toddler, her owner died. She and her family were passed to his son, Charles Hardenbergh. About five years later, Isabella was cruelly separated from her parents. The frightened and lonely nine-year-old child was sold at a slave auction for $100. Later she would remember that a flock of sheep was sold along with her, to increase her value to her new owner. She said that "her trails [trials] in life" began with this separation from her parents.

Her new owner was John Neely, who ran a small store in Kingston, New York. The young Isabella was the only slave Neely owned, which meant that she had to do all the work in the house and in the store. Neely and his wife spoke only English. Because Isabella was raised speaking Dutch, she could not understand the orders her owners gave her. She often was punished for not understanding

Sojourner Truth was taken away from her family and was auctioned off at the age of nine. She recalled in her *Narrative* that, to increase people's bids on her, sheep were thrown in as part of the deal. This oil painting by Ed Wong-Longda is a depiction of Isabella with the sheep.

Slavery began in New York with the arrival of the first Dutch settlers in 1626. Even after the English captured the colony on September 5, 1664, slavery continued. When Isabella was born, most families in Ulster County were of Dutch origin. They owned small farms where they grew wheat and raised sheep for wool. In New York and other northern states, most masters owned only a few slaves. This meant that the slaves in each household were isolated from each other. They couldn't develop friendships with other slaves or share their common African culture. Slaves in New York did not suffer the brutal living and working conditions endured by slaves in the South. However, the lack of freedom and human dignity was the same in both places. New York was one of the last northern states to abolish slavery. In 1799, the state adopted a series of gradual steps to free slaves. On July 4, 1827, all remaining adult slaves in the state were freed. Any slaves under age 18 in 1827 still had to remain in servitude until age 28 if they were male and age 25 if they were female.

In this hand-colored woodcut, slaves are shown working in the cotton field. Small children often stayed by their mothers' sides in the field, helping to gather the crop if they were old enough.

commands. Some of these beatings were so harsh that she carried the scars on her back for the rest of her life.

About a year later she was sold again, this time to Martin Schriver, a Dutch fisherman who also ran a tavern in Kingston, New York. Isabella did various types of work for Schriver, including making beer, shopping, hoeing corn, and gathering herbs in the woods.

Isabella spent only a little more than a year with the Schrivers before she was sold in 1810 to the Dumonts in New Paltz, New York. Once there, she finally stopped shifting from family to family. The Dumonts kept her for sixteen years. She worked both on the farm and in the house, doing general household chores. She also nursed members of the family when they were sick.

When she was a teenager, Isabella fell in love with a slave named Robert from a farm near the Dumonts'. Robert's owner objected to the match. He wanted his slaves to marry one another, so that legally he would own all of their children. Robert was beaten when he tried to visit Isabella and was finally forced to marry a slave from his own farm. Isabella was heartbroken when he stopped visiting her.

Soon after, Isabella married Tom, a fellow slave on the Dumont farm. This marriage was arranged by her master. They had five children together. One died in infancy, but Diana, Peter, Elizabeth, and Sophia all lived. Isabella sometimes took her children with her when she worked in the fields. She placed her baby in a basket hung from a tree, and the older children were set to work swinging the basket.

By 1835, all the northern states had passed laws to free the slaves still remaining within their borders. However, in New York State, slaves over age eighteen were to be freed on July 4, 1827. Children under eighteen had to wait until they were older. Isabella made a bargain with her master that she would be set free a year early, in 1826, if she did extra work on the farm.

When the time came, though, Dumont refused to honor his agreement. He said that Isabella had injured her hand and had not completed the extra work she had promised to do. Isabella thought she had kept her part of the deal. She was unusually tall at almost 6 feet (2 m), and she was strong for a woman. Isabella normally accomplished more than the average slave, even with an injured hand.

Wishing to be fair, however, Isabella stayed through the summer and the fall of 1826. On top of her regular tasks, she spun 100 pounds (45 kg) of wool, an entire winter's work. Finally, in the early winter, Isabella figured that she had done the necessary extra work to make up for being slowed by her injured hand. She decided to leave the Dumont farm and to find freedom.

Freedom was a new concept to Isabella, and she was not sure how to proceed. She told friends later, "I did not run off, for I thought that wicked, but I walked off, believing that to be all right." Early one morning, she packed up her few clothes and possessions and took off down the road, carrying her infant daughter, Sophia.

Her husband, Tom, and her older children remained on the Dumont farm. No one knows for sure why she left her other children behind. Perhaps she felt that they would be better cared for on the farm, as her own plans were so uncertain. Because her children were minors, by law they had to remain in slavery for many more years after Isabella walked to freedom.

She did not go far on that first journey away from slavery. She went just a few miles (km) down the road to the home of Isaac and Marie Van Wagenen, whom she had known for years. This family opposed slavery and offered to pay Isabella for her work if she chose to stay with them. When Dumont found her and tried to take her back into slavery, the Van Wagenens paid him $25 for Isabella's and Sophia's freedom for a year. Isabella adopted the last name of Van Wagenen and stayed for what she called a "quiet and peaceful" year with "these noble people." For the first time in her thirty-one years, Isabella was not afraid of being beaten by an angry master. She was free.

3. Living Free

During the year that Isabella lived with the Van Wagenen family, she had two life-changing experiences. The first was a powerful religious experience, stemming from a vision. Fighting in court for her son's freedom would be another milestone in her life.

Isabella had been taught about God's love as a young child at her mother's knee. Her mother had said, "My children, there is a God, who sees and hears you. When you are beaten, or cruelly treated, or fall into any trouble, you must ask for help of him and he will always hear and help you." Isabella's faith that God would always hear her helped her through many difficult moments.

Following her release from slavery, her life grew easier and she had less need to call on God. This all changed on June 4, 1827, as she prepared to celebrate the holiday of Pinkster. Pinkster was the Dutch name for Pentecost, the seventh Sunday after Easter. The blacks in New York also celebrated Pinkster as a carnival time, and they would gather to share their African American culture.

Pinkster is one of the oldest African American holidays in the United States and is the oldest in the New York area. It dates from the early Dutch colonial period in what is now New York and New Jersey. The week-long celebrations of Pinkster include the putting up of booths, the selling of goods, and much merrymaking through song and dance.

Isabella had a premonition that her former master, John Dumont, would come to the Van Wagenens to take her back to his farm for Pinkster. He did, in fact, come in a wagon, and Isabella prepared to go with him for the day. She was eager to celebrate the holiday with her slave friends. As she started to climb into Dumont's wagon, she had a powerful vision. She said, "God revealed himself, with all the suddenness of a flash of lightning." Isabella became aware of her "great sin in forgetting her almighty Friend" during the past year. She fainted, and when she recovered, Dumont was gone. She returned to the Van Wagenens' house, changed by her experience.

Isabella was filled with a new determination to honor God after her vision. She started to attend a Methodist church. It was one of the few types of churches that welcomed blacks at their services. Isabella also felt comfortable there, because the Methodists encouraged individuals to speak about their personal experiences with God.

Isabella's new peace was soon shattered. She learned that John Dumont had sold her five-year-old son, Peter, to a new owner. A few months later, Peter was sold again, this time south to Alabama. At that point, it was illegal to sell a minor slave, such as Peter, who would be freed once he reached age twenty-eight, out of the state of New York. This law was passed to prevent New York owners from selling young slaves to Southern owners, who would never free them.

Isabella feared she would never see her son again, and that he would spend the rest of his life in slavery. She had to bring him back to New York. Sure that God would help her, Isabella started her campaign to bring Peter back.

She went to the family who had sold her son and begged them for help. "My boy has gone as a slave and he is too little to go so far from his mother. Oh, I must have my child." They would not help.

Isabella realized that the only chance she had of getting Peter back was to go to court. Could a poor, black woman, an ex-slave unable to read or write, really expect help from the court system?

Friends told Isabella to seek aid from a nearby Quaker family. They helped her to find the county courthouse in Kingston. There she did something unusual for a poor woman. She told her story to the grand jury. A grand jury is a group of people who gather to evaluate the evidence against someone charged with a crime. After asking Isabella some questions, the grand jury believed her accusations against Peter's former owner and sent an order for the man to appear in court. He refused to come.

This is a recent photo of Ulster County Courthouse in Kingston, New York. Truth addressed the jury about her son Peter in this building. She won the case against his former owner, making her the first African American woman to win a case against a white man.

After almost a year, Peter was brought back from Alabama, because his former owner feared that the court eventually would rule against him. He still refused to let Isabella see her son, though. After months of delay, Peter was finally brought to court. Isabella was horrified to see the scars on his face and body.

The judge decided that Peter should live with his mother. Isabella was heartbroken when the boy did not recognize her. It had been about two years since the six-year-old child had last seen his mother. In addition, he was suffering emotionally from having been severely beaten in Alabama. He came to live with her, but it took many months before he accepted Isabella as his mother.

The one bright spot in the tragic story was that Peter was free. Because he had been illegally sold south, the court said that he did not have to wait until he was twenty-eight to be released from slavery. Two of Isabella's daughters were still bound to their masters, but at least she had her son, Peter, and her baby, Sophia, with her.

In 1827 and in 1828, a series of dramatic events had occurred in Isabella's life. She had walked away from slavery, had experienced a religious vision, had battled successfully in court to recover her son, and had found a spiritual home in a new church. She was now ready to discover an even wider world.

Isabella decided to move to New York City with some Methodist friends. It is not known where the baby Sophia went at this time. Isabella's other daughters had to stay with the Dumonts in New Paltz, New York, until their term of slavery ended. However, Isabella took Peter with her to New York City. A fairly large population of free blacks lived there at this time. There were black schools, newspapers, and churches. After attending the segregated John Street Methodist Church, Isabella soon joined the Zion Methodist Church, a largely black congregation. There she saw her sister Sophia, after whom she had named her daughter. Sophia introduced her to their brother, Michael. Isabella had never known either of them as children, because they had been sold away from the family before she was even born.

Gradually Isabella and some of her friends moved away from the traditional Methodist church to a more informal group. The Free Methodists opposed slavery and encouraged women to become preachers. In this new group, Isabella met some abolitionists, who were passionate opponents of slavery. She became known as a forceful preacher at revival meetings. Her testimony about the powerful love of God converted many listeners. Isabella developed an imposing style of public speaking, using her unusual height to command attention on the stage. She found that her strong, low voice had a powerful effect on audiences.

As part of her religious work in New York City, Isabella helped young, homeless white and black women at the Magdalene Asylum. She taught them skills, such as cooking, sewing, and cleaning, to help them find work as servants. While at the asylum, she met the director, a white man named Elijah Pierson. She came to admire Pierson and his wife, Sarah, for their religious passion.

Following spread: This 1849 picture of New York City was made by Henry A. Papprill. When Sojourner Truth moved there in 1828, she brought a paper certifying her conversion to Methodism. This paper enabled her to join New York's John Street Methodist Church.

Through the Piersons, Isabella met Robert Matthias, the forty-year-old white leader of a religious cult. Matthias claimed to be a prophet who could forgive sins, for a small fee. He wore long, flowing robes and left his hair and beard untrimmed to appear more like Jesus.

Isabella fell under the spell of this charismatic preacher. She moved into his home and worked as his housekeeper. She became the only black member of the small group of followers that Matthias called his kingdom. Both Elijah and Sarah Pierson also joined the kingdom. Matthias and the fifteen to twenty members

This is a picture of Robert Matthias. His authoritative manner attracted audiences in the streets and churches where he preached. Matthias carried a key that symbolized his power to welcome or to expel people from a holy city that did not yet exist, called New Jerusalem.

> *In a commune, people put
> together their money and possessions.
> No one owns anything individually and all
> benefit equally from the shared wealth. Each
> member of the commune works at an
> assigned job, such as cooking, cleaning, or
> raising plants and animals for food, but
> no one is paid wages.*

of his kingdom moved north to Sing Sing, New York, and started a commune.

Isabella lived with the Kingdom of Matthias from 1832 to 1834. During these years, the group's behavior stirred up controversy. Members of the kingdom practiced communal bathing. Matthias whipped members when they disobeyed his rules. Matthias claimed he had the power to make and to dissolve marriages, "matching souls" of men and women he thought should be together. Their neighbors heard rumors of these actions and considered commune members to be rather peculiar.

In 1834, Elijah Pierson died while staying at the commune. Matthias was suspected of poisoning Pierson, because Matthias had refused to let doctors treat Pierson when he was ill. There was an investigation, but no formal charges were made right away.

After this scandal, the kingdom gradually fell apart, and the members went their separate ways. A few months later, new questions were raised about Pierson's death, and murder charges were finally brought against Matthias. He was tried eventually for murder but was acquitted because not enough evidence could be produced against him. Isabella remained loyal to Matthias throughout this difficult period in his life.

Some bad feelings had arisen toward Matthias within the commune, largely because of to his practice of "matching souls." Because of Isabella's complete loyalty to Matthias, certain commune members disliked her, too. After Matthias's trial, some former members of the kingdom started spreading rumors about Isabella. She was accused of helping Matthias to poison Pierson. A New York newspaper printed a story that described her as an "evil witch" responsible for breaking up the kingdom.

Isabella was very upset by these charges. She asked her former employers for letters stating that she was a dedicated and a loyal worker, as well as a person of "extraordinary moral purity." Even this measure did not stop the rumors.

For the second time in her life, Isabella turned to the courts for help. To clear her name, she sued the former kingdom members for slander. She told her lawyer, "I have got the truth, and I know it, and I will crush them with the truth." She was right, for she won her slander suit and was awarded $125 in damages, a large sum at the time, plus court costs.

Shaken by her experience in the Kingdom of Matthias, Isabella spent the next few years living quietly in New York City. She worked as a house servant, hoping to save enough money to buy a house of her own where she could live with her children.

4. The Sojourn Begins

After her return from the Kingdom of Matthias, the first problem Isabella faced was the unpromising future of her son, Peter. As a teenager, he had started to show signs of being a troublemaker. He went through several jobs but never stayed long at any of them. He studied navigation but skipped classes to go dancing. He was picked up by police several times for minor theft and finally was jailed.

Isabella recognized that she was not an ideal parent. She was too busy working to spend much time with her children, and she did not know how to lead them into good behavior. She also noticed that Peter had "little power to withstand temptation."

At her wit's end, Isabella agreed to send Peter to sea on a whaling ship. This was typical treatment for juvenile delinquents in that period. It was thought that time spent at sea, under the tough discipline of a ship captain, would straighten out any boy. In 1839, when Peter was eighteen years old, he boarded the ship *Zone*. From the ship, he wrote several letters home to his

Truth's son Peter boarded a whaling ship, like the one shown above, in 1839. The crews on these ships worked to catch whales and to extract useful products from them, such as oil.

This engraving by Benjamin Tanner from about 1810 shows the coast near the island of Nantucket, an area where Truth's son Peter did some whaling. The engraving is part of the Phelps Stokes Collection at the New York Public Library.

mother. Then he was never heard from again.

Except for her difficulties with Peter, very little is known of Isabella's life in New York for the nine years after her 1834 departure from the Kingdom of Matthias. She had a variety of jobs, usually as a domestic servant or a housekeeper. It is also known that she had become unhappy with life in the city. She was convinced that everything she had undertaken in New York was a failure. No matter how hard she worked, she had been unable to set aside any money. Convinced that the city was evil, she felt she must leave it.

On June 1, 1843, Isabella told her stunned employer that she "felt called in spirit to leave the city, and to travel east and lecture." When asked why, she replied simply, "The Spirit calls me there and I must go."

She announced that her name was to be Sojourner, meaning one who travels. She adopted Truth as her last name, because she intended to tell the truth to all who would listen. The former Isabella planned to become an itinerant preacher, spreading the word of God.

When she first lived in New York City, Isabella had done some public speaking and preaching as a member of the Methodist church. Although it was unusual for a woman, either black or white, to speak in public, it was not unheard of. Most of the other female preachers were associated with a church and traveled under the protection of that church. Isabella, however, preferred to remain independent.

With the exception of her short ventures in communal living, she did not join organizations, even if she agreed with their ideas. In 1843, the newly named Sojourner Truth proposed to set out on her own, unconnected to a specific denomination or organization. Traveling was potentially dangerous for a lone woman. She would have to find her own place to stay each night and could not rely on members of a church to provide safe lodging, because she did not belong to any denomination.

Truth left New York City carrying a small bundle of her possessions, a basket of food, and only two shillings (about 25 cents) in her purse. Her faith was strong that the Lord would guide her, protect her, and provide for her. Her mission was to "lecture, testifying of the hope that was in her."

In the early 1840s, a number of religious people were convinced that the end of the world was near. This belief was based on a complicated set of calculations

Starting in the 1840s, people from a religious group called the Millerites gathered at camp meetings to talk about the end of the world and the Second Coming of Jesus. Campsites were located where there was plenty of shade, grass, and clean water. The meeting shown in this drawing took place in Eastham, Massachusetts, in 1852.

about dates taken from the Bible. Itinerant preachers traveled around the country to prepare people for the Second Coming of Jesus. It was thought that during the Second Coming Christ would return to Earth to judge people and to determine whether they would go to heaven or to hell.

William Miller was one of the leaders who believed that the Second Coming was approaching. His followers were called Millerites. They held large outdoor gatherings, called camp meetings, around New York

William Miller predicted the world would end in 1843, then said it would end in 1844. He spread his belief to large audiences.

State and in New England. Truth preached at several Millerite camp meetings in New York and throughout New England.

Truth, however, was never convinced that she was truly a Millerite herself. An incident in Stepney, Connecticut, convinced her that she was not in complete sympathy with the group. It also illustrated one of Truth's talents as a speaker. She could quiet an unruly mob with simple common sense, delivered calmly and with humor.

The fiery speaker John Starkweather was addressing a Millerite camp meeting. Pacing up and down the aisles, waving a tree branch, and shouting "Glory," Starkweather threatened his listeners with eternal damnation if they did not give up all worldly items. He sincerely believed the Second Coming was near. His agitated listeners began to shed all of their symbols of vanity: clothing, jewelry, and even false teeth.

Truth was disgusted by the hysteria of the crowd. She mounted a tree stump and called out, "Hear! Hear!" to the Millerites. Some of the people gathered

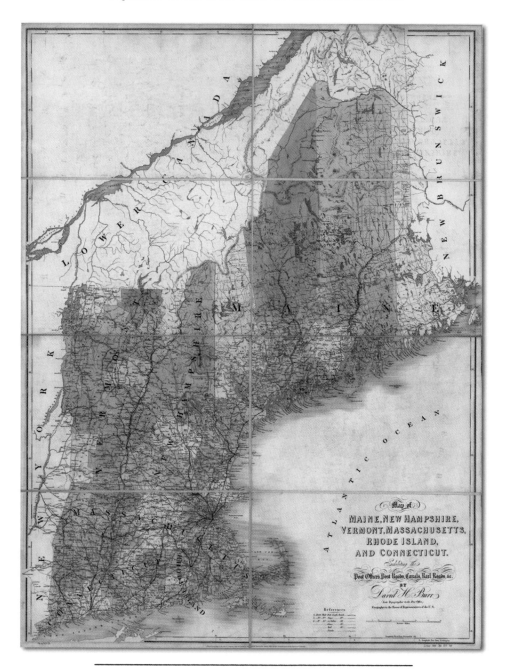

This 1839 map by David H. Burr shows the northeastern region of the United States known as New England, which includes Maine, New Hampshire, Vermont, Massachusetts, Rhode Island, and Connecticut. Sojourner Truth started traveling in this region in 1843 to attend Millerite camp meetings, where she spoke about the importance of faith in God.

around her as she tried to calm them. Using what would become one of her trademarks, she called them "my children," asking them why they were so excited. She told them to return to their tents and "watch and pray" quietly, "for the Lord would not come to such a scene of confusion."

Later Truth went to Starkweather and to other preachers in the camp. She scolded them for describing a scene in which all the wicked would burn in the fires of the Lord and the righteous would return to a purified world.

As she gained experience in preaching, she gained confidence in her ability to hold an audience. She also gained confidence in her own interpretation of God's will. She came to believe that God was an "all-powerful, all-pervading spirit" who spoke to her directly. She no longer needed the guidance of a preacher like Matthias to help her to understand God's will. Because she had never learned to read, Truth had the Bible read to her by her friends.

As Truth traveled through New England, she began drawing crowds and holding her own meetings. She enjoyed performing before an audience and reported that she was having a "good time" in her travels.

The Millerites continued to invite her to speak at their meetings, which she did frequently throughout New England in the fall of 1843. She told her listeners that God loved each of them and that their faith in this love would change their lives.

In delivering this message over and over, Truth perfected her own singular style of preaching. She became known for "her commanding figure and dignified manner." She used everyday language and folk humor in her speeches. Truth always loved singing and frequently used hymns in her preaching. Her deep, rich voice made her a favorite with audiences, who responded to her gift for praying and for singing.

As Truth went from town to town in New England, she sought food and lodging wherever she could find it. A friend described her travels, "Wherever night overtook her, there she sought for lodgings—free if she might—if not, she paid; at a tavern, if she chanced to be at one—if not, at a private dwelling; with the rich if they would receive her—if not, with the poor."

By the beginning of winter 1843, Truth was ready to stop traveling and to find lodging for the season. There was a commune in Northampton, Massachusetts, that seemed a good place to stay the winter. It had a reputation for moderate beliefs and was not run by fanatics. This came as a relief to Truth, who had been hurt by her experience with the Kingdom of Matthias.

Opposite: Sojourner Truth became a powerful and an influential voice for social reform in nineteenth-century America. She captivated audiences around the country as she spoke out against slavery and advocated for women's rights.

5. The Northampton Association

When Sojourner Truth joined the Northampton Association for Education and Industry in 1843, there were thirty men, twenty-six women, and forty-six children living in the community. The group, which included both black and white families, planned to manufacture and sell silk to support its residents.

They lived simply in one large, four-story stone building, which also served as the silk factory. The rooms were simple and the residents bathed in the nearby river. A variety of livestock, including horses, oxen, pigs, cows, and poultry, shared the 500-acre (202-ha) site with the residential building, the grist, and the saw mills.

The liberal community welcomed blacks as members. Everyone was assigned a job and all were paid six cents per hour for their labor. From these wages, each adult paid fifty cents each week for board and for lodging. Truth was soon placed in charge of the laundry, located in the basement of the factory building. As did all the residents, she worked twelve hours per day and ate in the common dining room. Lights were out at 10:00 P.M.

Although the Northampton residents worked hard and lived simply, there was much intellectual activity in the community. There were libraries and reading rooms for the residents, who prided themselves on their intellectual exchange. Visiting lecturers included the most famous social reformers of the period.

It was here that Truth first met leading abolitionists and supporters of rights for women. As she listened to and talked with these passionate reformers, Truth found herself agreeing with their ideas.

She became lifelong friends with several of the leaders she met at Northampton. Frederick Douglass was another former slave who had become a powerful public speaker. He had been born into slavery in Maryland and had escaped to Massachusetts as a young man. When he met Truth at Northampton, he was traveling as a lecturer for the Massachusetts Anti-Slavery Society. Douglass was an occasional visitor to the commune, and he and Truth became friends over many months.

William Lloyd Garrison was another frequent visitor to the commune. He was the editor of the famous abolitionist newspaper, *The Liberator*. Garrison founded the American Anti-Slavery Society and traveled with Douglass giving antislavery lectures.

In 1845, while Truth was at Northampton, Frederick Douglass published his autobiography,

This painting of the American writer and abolitionist Frederick Douglass was made by Elisha Hammond around 1844. Douglass, an escaped slave, bought his freedom with money earned from lecturing after the publication of his first autobiography.

NARRATIVE

OF THE

LIFE

OF

FREDERICK DOUGLASS,

AN

AMERICAN SLAVE.

WRITTEN BY HIMSELF.

BOSTON:
PUBLISHED AT THE ANTI-SLAVERY OFFICE,
No. 25 CORNHILL
1845.

The title page from the *Narrative of the Life of Frederick Douglass, An American Slave* faces an engraved portrait of its author. The book was published by the Anti-Slavery Office in Boston in 1845.

Slave narratives were books written or told by escaped or former slaves. The standard book gave graphic descriptions of the abuses of slavery. They often included the upsetting details of an escape. These stories were used by abolitionists to whip up reaction against slavery. When the authors were on the lecture circuit, they often removed their shirts to show the scars from beatings. Some narratives became best-sellers. The most famous one was written by Frederick Douglass in 1845. His autobiography, Narrative of the Life of Frederick Douglass, An American Slave, *sold 4,500 copies in less than six months.*

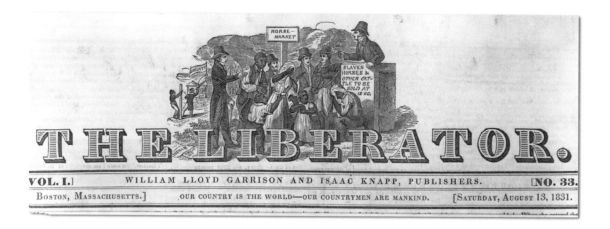

THE LIBERATOR.

VOL. I.]   WILLIAM LLOYD GARRISON AND ISAAC KNAPP, PUBLISHERS.   [NO. 33.

BOSTON, MASSACHUSETTS.]   OUR COUNTRY IS THE WORLD—OUR COUNTRYMEN ARE MANKIND.   [SATURDAY, AUGUST 13, 1831.

This is the masthead of the Boston antislavery newspaper *The Liberator*. The May 1850 issue of this paper ran an advertisement by its editor, William Lloyd Garrison, promoting Sojourner Truth's book. Garrison published *The Liberator* from 1831 until after the end of the Civil War in 1865. He used passionate language in his newspaper to support the immediate freeing of all slaves and to advocate for their legal equality in every way with the United States's white citizens.

Narrative of the Life of Frederick Douglass, An American Slave. The book was printed by William Lloyd Garrison. Douglass's book was one of several slave narratives published in this period. Such books, describing the horrors of slavery and arguing for the freedom of slaves, were popular with abolitionists.

While Truth was at Northampton, she went to a nearby outdoor camp meeting. A group of wild young men interrupted the meeting. They started yelling at the speakers and even threatened to burn the tents. The leaders called the police, which only infuriated the rioters. They roamed the campgrounds, shaking tents and terrifying the worshipers. Truth feared for her life and hid behind a trunk in a tent. She said to herself, "I am the only colored person here, and on me, probably, their wicked mischief will fall first, and perhaps fatally." Then she began asking herself why she was afraid, when she was "the servant of the living God. Have I not faith enough to go out and quell that mob?"

No one else was willing to go with her to face the rioters, so Truth went alone. She walked to the top of a nearby hill and started to sing one of her favorite hymns. She was soon surrounded by the young men. As they pressed around her, she stopped singing and asked, "Why do you come about me with clubs and sticks? I am not doing harm to anyone."

"We aren't going to hurt you, old woman; we came to hear you sing," cried voices from the crowd. Sojourner climbed on top of a wagon and began preaching to the young men. For over an hour she spoke and sang. This served to calm the rioters, who listened with

Truth preached at this podium in the First Presbyterian Church in Coldwater, Michigan.

increasing attention. Finally, she grew weary and asked if the group would leave the campgrounds if she sang one more song. The crowd agreed and departed peacefully as she sang.

Truth had clearly become a powerful and a persuasive speaker, skilled in handling a crowd. She would use this ability in the future, as she faced larger and more skeptical audiences.

6. On the Lecture Circuit

The Northampton Association for Education and Industry dissolved in 1846, largely for financial reasons. During the three years Truth spent there, she met some leaders of the reform movement for abolition and women's suffrage. She adopted the movements' messages as her own. She was painfully aware of the restrictions imposed on slaves and on women. In addition to preaching God's love, as she had in the past, Truth spoke to audiences in more than twenty states about rights for slaves and for women.

While she was at the Northampton Association, Truth met a white woman named Olive Gilbert. Truth's history impressed Gilbert, an abolitionist friend of William Lloyd Garrison's. A few years later, the two women worked together to create the *Narrative of Sojourner Truth.* Because Truth was illiterate, she could not write her own story. Instead, she told her story to Gilbert, who transformed their conversations into a short, 125-page book.

SOJOURNER TRUTH,

"THE LIBYAN SIBYL."

NARRATIVE

OF

SOJOURNER TRUTH;

A Bondswoman of Olden Time,

EMANCIPATED BY THE NEW YORK LEGISLATURE IN THE EARLY
PART OF THE PRESENT CENTURY;

WITH A HISTORY OF HER

Labors and Correspondence,

DRAWN FROM HER

"BOOK OF LIFE."

———•———

BOSTON:
PUBLISHED FOR THE AUTHOR.
1875.

Truth never learned to read or write. This is the only known example of her signature, dated April 23, 1880, from an autograph book belonging to a local schoolgirl named Hattie Johnson.

Truth borrowed $500 to print her *Narrative* from William Lloyd Garrison, who had published Frederick Douglass's autobiography. Garrison added a testimonial at the end of the book, calling Truth a "most remarkable and highly meritorious woman." The book helped make her name and story more familiar to the public. The attention was good for her career as a nationwide lecturer, which was not yet at its peak.

In 1850, when the *Narrative* was published, Truth was fifty-three years old. She wore glasses and her black hair had turned to gray. She wore a long, white shawl over a simple, black dress. A handkerchief was wrapped around her head like a turban. Many people thought she looked older than her years, but her appearance was deceiving. She spoke with great force and vigor.

After the Northampton Association closed, Truth needed a place to live. For a while she lived and worked in the home of George Benson, a former member of the

Previous spread: Narrative of Sojourner Truth, first published in 1850 in Boston and in New York, reveals the life of a black northerner in the early to mid-nineteenth century. It helped to illustrate the horrors of slavery and to advance the abolitionist movement.

I Sell the Shadow to Support the Substance.

Sojourner Truth sold these portraits of herself to raise money while she traveled on lecture tours. The caption at the bottom refers to Truth's shadow, or photograph, being the means by which she supported herself financially.

Association. When his cotton mill went bankrupt, she was once again homeless. It had been her long-held dream to own "a little home of her own." She had never had the money to make this dream a reality.

Another former member of the Association came to her rescue. In 1850, at the same time that the *Narrative* was published, Samuel Hill built a house for Truth in Northampton. He sold her the house for $300 and gave her a mortgage for the full amount.

For the first time in her life, Truth had a home of her own. However, she now owed money for the first time, both to the printer of her book and to the builder of her home. Determined to pay off her debts quickly, she started a new lecture tour around the country and sold her book to raise money. She sold the *Narrative* for 25 cents, which was an unusually low price for a book in this period. Perhaps Truth kept the price low to encourage more people to buy it.

In 1850, Truth gave one of her first speeches on her new lecture tour to the National Women's Rights Convention in Worcester, Massachusetts. Several of her Northampton friends were also at this meeting, which was one of the early women's rights meetings held in the United States.

The very first gathering of women's rights supporters had been held only two years earlier in Seneca Falls, New York. There, for the first time, women united to fight for expansion of their opportunities. In the

1840s and 1850s, women could not vote or hold political office. Few women received an education, and they were not considered intelligent enough to deal with academic or abstract ideas.

The lives and the property of unmarried women were under the control of their fathers or brothers. After a woman married, control of her money and property was turned over to her husband. Most women did not work outside the home; if they did, they were paid considerably less than men. Women were not allowed to sue for divorce, although men could divorce their wives at will. After a divorce, the husband retained custody of the children.

Some of the first women to argue publicly for women's rights were originally abolitionists. Several pioneers, such as Lucretia Mott and Susan B. Anthony, learned to run meetings, to organize petition drives, and to appear on public platforms as they fought the evils of slavery. They used this experience to establish the movement for women's rights.

Sojourner Truth soon joined the ranks of speakers for women's rights. At the 1850 convention, she listened as Elizabeth Cady Stanton, Lucretia Mott, Frederick Douglass, and William Lloyd Garrison spoke. Finally it was her turn. She rose and began in her usual direct fashion: "Sisters, I ain't clear what you be after. If women want any rights more than they's got, why don't they just take them, and not be talking about it?"

This is a photo of Susan B. Anthony, a famous women's rights activist. She cofounded the National Women's Loyal League in 1863.

It was not that simple. One of the major problems was that many men were strongly opposed to granting women any political or economic rights. Either they feared what would happen if women could do more, or they honestly believed that women could not handle any more responsibility.

The women themselves were divided on how to achieve their goals. Some wanted to use the legal system to gain their rights through lawsuits. Others thought that pressuring politicians would be more effective.

Truth's lecture tour as an abolitionist and a women's rights supporter began in 1850. William Lloyd Garrison invited her to accompany him and the abolitionist George Thompson on a tour of western New York State. The money Truth earned selling her book at her appearances would help her pay off the loan she'd received from Garrison to print the *Narrative*.

While she was on the road, Truth stayed with friends to help lower expenses. In the spring of 1851, Truth decided to arrange her own lecture tour in Ohio. She stayed with Marius and Emily Robinson, who lived in Salem, Ohio. Marius Robinson was the president of the Western Anti-Slavery Society and editor of the *Anti-Slavery Bugle* newspaper. The Ohio Women's Rights Convention met in Akron in May 1851. Frances Dana Gage, a writer, presided. The three-day meeting welcomed men and women, white and black, who favored women's rights. It was on this lecture tour that Truth made one of her most famous speeches.

Truth came forward and said: "I am [for] woman's rights. I have as much muscle as any man, and can do as much work as any man. I have plowed and reaped and husked and chopped and mowed, and can man do any more than that? I have heard much about the sexes being equal; I can carry as much as any man, and can eat as much, too, if I can get it. I am as strong as any man that is now."

Truth also used a biblical argument to reinforce her point. "I can't read, but I can hear. I have heard the Bible and have learned that Eve caused man to sin. Well, if woman upset the world, do give her a chance to set it right side up again . . . And how came Jesus into the world? Through God who created him and woman who bore him. Man, where is your part?"

This speech illustrates the power of Truth's words. She used everyday, familiar images to make her point. She did not argue abstract philosophy, but spoke directly about the daily life of her audience.

Her appearance at the Akron convention helped Truth become better known to national leaders of reform movements. She dictated in a letter to her friend Amy Post, who had helped to arrange a women's rights convention in 1848, that she had met "plenty of kind friends just like you and they gave me so many kind invitations I hardly knew which to accept of first." Truth's future on the lecture circuit seemed assured. She also sold enough copies of the *Narrative* to send Garrison $50 toward the printing bill.

For the next several years, Truth traveled to almost every northern state, speaking for abolition and for women's rights. She traveled by railroad from town to town. Because she was illiterate, Truth frequently had a companion to help with the travel arrangements. For several years, she was accompanied by her grandson Sammy Banks. He was the son of her middle daughter,

Elizabeth. Following the death of Sammy in 1875, Sojourner needed a new travel companion. So she asked Frances Titus, her Quaker friend from Battle Creek, Michigan, to go with her on the lecture tours. Companions such as Titus helped Truth by reading to her, arranging train schedules, writing letters, taking care of finances, and placing notices in the newspaper.

Frances Titus was editor of the 1870s and 1880s editions of the *Narrative of Sojourner Truth*. She was Truth's traveling companion from 1867 until Truth's death in 1883. Titus was an abolitionist, a suffragist, and an advocate for the rights of the oppressed.

Sojourner Truth's friends and sponsors took care of her travel and living costs, either through gifts or loans. Frances Titus wrote a typical appeal to her supporters. "She is much in need of present assistance. . . . She wishes me to say to you if loan or collection could be forwarded to her from Detroit, of $30, she will come out, hold meetings and sell her photographs, and by such means refund the money, after a few weeks."

Sojourner Truth sold portraits of herself to raise money for living expenses and to pay her debts. These portraits, which usually measured about 3 inches high by 2 inches across (8 x 5 cm), were known as cartes-de-visite, *the French phrase for "calling cards." The process for making* cartes-de-visite *was invented in the 1850s. It became possible to take a number of small pictures in a single negative and to print many inexpensive copies. Because it was economical, the process quickly gained wide use in Europe and the United States, starting in the mid-1860s. Politicians, actors, authors, and lecturers used the* cartes-de-visite *for publicity, as a sort of combination of today's baseball card and business card of today. Abolitionists sold cards showing slaves' bodies, scarred from whippings. Unlike some antislavery activists, Truth chose images that showed her as an intelligent, middle-class matron, sitting by a fireplace knitting or holding a book. There are no visible reminders that she was once a slave, and no attempt is made to create pity for her former plight.*

To raise money to pay off her debts and loans, Truth continued to sell the *Narrative*. She increased the price of the book from 25 cents to 50 cents after a second edition was printed in 1855. Sometimes she sold sheets with the words to her favorite songs for 5 or 10 cents each.

In the mid-1850s, she added another item to sell at her lectures. She had photographs taken and made into *cartes-de-visite*, or calling cards. Under the picture was written, "I sell the shadow to support the substance." She meant that she sold the picture of herself, the shadow, to support her body, the substance. The small cards sold for 33 cents each. A larger size, approximately 4 by 6 inches (10 x 15 cm), cost 50 cents.

Truth's dream to own a home had been realized in 1850. By 1854, she had raised enough money to pay off the entire mortgage of her Northampton home. It is ironic that she could not spend much time in her house, because she was traveling on the lecture circuit for months at a time.

7. The Battle Creek Years

In 1856, one of Truth's trips took her to Battle Creek, a village in southwestern Michigan with strong Quaker roots. She spoke to the Friends of Human Progress, a radical Quaker abolitionist group, and must have liked what she saw of the settlement. The next year, she sold her house in Northampton and returned to the Battle Creek area. She bought land and built a home in the nearby village of Harmonia.

It is not known for certain why Truth chose to leave her Massachusetts home and move to Michigan. Perhaps it was because the tolerant atmosphere created by the Quakers made her feel comfortable. The Quakers were a small religious denomination who believed that all points of view should be valued. They had been subject to persecution in the past and were determined that they would not allow any other group to feel this pain. Quakers were also active social reformers. They strongly supported abolition and rights for women, two of Truth's favorite causes.

Perhaps Truth came to the Battle Creek area because she already knew one of the families who lived

This was downtown Battle Creek, Michigan, as Truth saw it in the late 1850s and 1860s. Truth spoke in the Quaker Meeting House, which was located in this area.

in Harmonia. Dorcas and Reynolds Cornell had lived in Ulster County, New York, and had known Truth while she was still the slave Isabella. Dorcas Cornell's parents had been members of the Quaker group that helped Isabella recover her son, Peter.

This was her third and final venture into communal living. Harmonia was not a structured commune but a group of Quakers and Spiritualists who formed a loose association of families sharing common beliefs.

Her life in Harmonia probably brought special

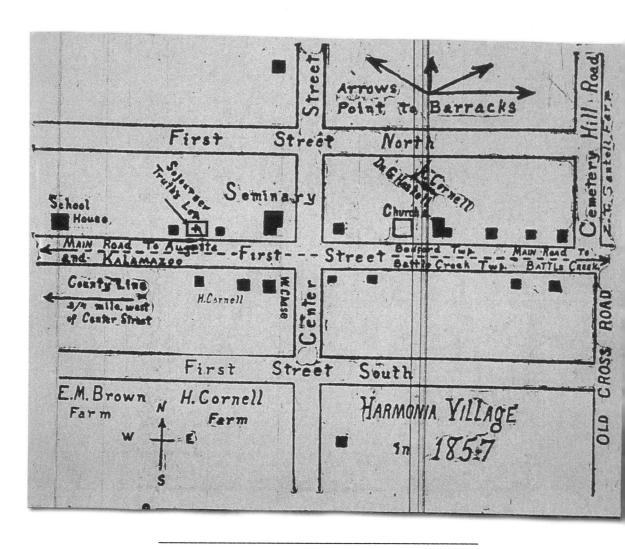

When Truth moved to Michigan in 1857,
she bought land in Harmonia Village. This map
shows the village as it appeared in 1857. Sojourner Truth's lot is
outlined in red.

In 1848, a new sensation called Spiritualism swept across the country. Spiritualists were members of a religion that thought that the human personality continues to exist after death and can communicate with the living through a medium. A medium is an individual believed to be a channel of communication between this world and the world of spirits.

Most organized religious groups attacked the Spiritualists, ridiculing their idea of communication with the dead. The social reformers were split on the issue. Some, like Frederick Douglass and Lucretia Mott, did not believe in Spiritualism. Others, including William Lloyd Garrison, felt the new religion reinforced the Christian belief in immortality. Most radical Quaker groups, including the Friends of Human Progress, accepted Spiritualism. By the 1860s, progressive Quakerism and Spiritualism had become almost completely intermingled. As the movement became more popular, con artists tried to fake communication with spirits. When their tricks were revealed, the Spiritualist movement lost credibility. By the 1870s, the wide popularity of the Spiritualist movement began to decline.

Truth moved to Battle Creek, Michigan, in 1867 and owned the house at 38 College Street until her death in 1883. This drawing of her house in Battle Creek appeared in a local newspaper in 1908. It was taken from a Chicago newspaper dating from the 1890s. There are no surviving photos of the house.

comfort to Truth. For the first time in many years, Truth had most of her family living around her. Her three daughters, now grown and married, moved to the Battle Creek area to be with their mother. Truth would be able to enjoy watching her grandchildren grow up around her.

The settlement at Harmonia gradually broke apart, though. Several families moved away, and Truth might have become uncomfortable with some of the Spiritualists who did not embrace social reforms. In 1867, she moved into Battle Creek itself, buying a barn and a lot on College Street. She went to work fixing up a couple of rooms to live in for the winter.

When her house was finally completed, it was not spacious or elaborate. A visiting friend described it as "a miserable little house, of two rooms—the one contains her cot also. . . . the cook stove, which with a chair or two took up all the space." She could be seen "smoking a clay pipe usually—in front of her dwelling, on a little platform, every evening in the summer at the close of day."

During the twenty-six years that she lived in Harmonia and in Battle Creek, Truth continued to travel around the nation delivering her message of

Tobacco pouches are used to hold pipes and tobacco, keeping pipes clean and tobacco moist and flavorful. This tobacco pouch is one of Truth's few surviving personal possessions. In 1917, it was donated to the state museum in Lansing, Michigan.

This is a photo of Truth's daughter Diana Corbin.
Corbin died in the county poorhouse in 1904. She is
buried beside her mother in Battle Creek, Michigan.

reform. In fact, she was gone from the city for many months at a time. She still regarded the Michigan village as her home, and the citizens were proud of their "distinguished townswoman."

Truth became a local tourist attraction, and notable visitors were taken to meet her. An attorney remembered that the mayor "took me out driving, to see the sights of the town, and asked me if I would like to meet Sojourner Truth. Naturally I wanted to call on her, as she was then known all over the country, looked upon as a most remarkable woman."

Truth's sense of humor sometimes led her to tease these guests. She exaggerated her age to enhance her reputation as the "world's oldest lecturer." On occasion she might have tricked her visitors by having her daughter Diana, who looked remarkably like Truth, greet them in her place.

8. The Legend Grows

Between 1850 and 1863, Sojourner Truth's reputation was growing among abolitionists and women's rights advocates. She was not yet widely known by the general public. Then, in the spring of 1863, two articles were published that made her a national celebrity. Both stories gave a very inaccurate picture of Truth, but they made her famous.

One story was written by Harriet Beecher Stowe, author of the famous 1852 antislavery novel, *Uncle Tom's Cabin*. Stowe's article on Truth appeared in the April 1863 edition of the *Atlantic Monthly*, then one of the most respected and widely read magazines in the country.

Stowe had met Truth only once, back in 1853, when Truth had traveled to the author's home in Andover, Massachusetts, to ask her to write a favorable review of the *Narrative*. In the late 1850s, while Stowe was traveling in Rome, Italy, she met a sculptor named William Wetmore Story and mentioned her encounter with Sojourner Truth.

This is a photo of Harriet Beecher Stowe. Stowe is perhaps best known for her antislavery novel *Uncle Tom's Cabin*, but she also wrote for local and religious periodicals and authored poems, travel books, biographical sketches, and children's books.

SOJOURNER TRUTH, THE LIBYAN SIBYL.

MANY years ago, the few readers of radical Abolitionist papers must often have seen the singular name of Sojourn-er Truth, announced as a frequent speaker at Anti-Slavery meetings, and as travelling on a sort of self-appointed agency through the country. I had myself often remarked the name, but never met the individual. On one occasion, when our house was filled with company, several eminent clergymen being our guests, notice was brought up to me that Sojourner Truth was below, and requested an interview. Knowing nothing of her but her singular name, I went down, prepared to make the interview short, as the pressure of many other engagements demanded.

When I went into the room, a tall, spare form arose to meet me. She was evidently a full-blooded African, and though now aged and worn with many hardships, still gave the impression of a physical development which in early youth must have been as fine a specimen of the torrid zone as Cumberworth's celebrated statuette of the Negro Wom- at the Fountain. Indeed, she so strongly reminded me of that figure, that, when I recall the events of her life, as she narrated them to me, I imagine her as a living, breathing impersonation of that work of art.

I do not recollect ever to have been conversant with any one who had more of that silent and subtle power which we call personal presence than this woman. In the modern Spiritualistic phraseology, she would be described as having a strong sphere. Her tall form, as she rose up before me, is still vivid to my mind. She was dressed in some stout, grayish stuff, neat and clean, though dusty from trav-el. On her head she wore a bright Madras handkerchief, arranged as a turban, after the manner of her race. She seemed perfectly self-possessed and at her ease, — in fact, there was almost an unconscious superiority, not unmixed with a solemn twinkle of humor, in the odd, composed manner in which she looked down on me. Her whole air had at times a gloomy sort of drollery which impressed one strangely.

" So, this is you," she said.

" Yes," I answered.

" Well, honey, de Lord bless ye! I jes' thought I 'd like to come an' have a look at ye. You 's heerd o' me, I reckon?" she added.

" Yes, I think I have. You go about lecturing, do you not?"

" Yes, honey, that 's what I do. The Lord has made me a sign unto this nation, an' I go round a-testifyin', an' showin' on 'em their sins agin my people."

So saying, she took a seat, and, stooping over and crossing her arms on her knees, she looked down on the floor, and appeared to fall into a sort of reverie

---

This is Harriet Beecher Stowe's 1863 *Atlantic Monthly* article on Sojourner Truth. The article described a romanticized version of Sojourner Truth. Unfortunately, many people began to think of Truth as the two-dimensional Libyan Sybil described in the article.

At that time, Story was working on a series of large statues of the sibyls, female characters from Greek and Roman mythology. When he heard about Truth and the life she led, he was beginning his Libyan, or African, sibyl. Although he had never met Truth, he was inspired by Stowe's description and created an imaginary picture of Truth to use as a model for his sculpture.

The statue, which was completed in 1860, did not look at all like Truth. However, the artist never intended his image to be accurate. He considered his work an "anti-slavery sermon in stone." Three years later, Harriet Beecher Stowe would take the statue's name for the title of her *Atlantic Monthly* article on Truth, "Sojourner Truth, the Libyan Sibyl."

Stowe loosely based her article on the visit that Truth had paid to her a decade earlier. Although she told the basic facts of Truth's story, Stowe romanticized almost every aspect of Truth's life. She described Truth as a "native African woman" who spoke with a strong dialect. Truth's grandparents had come from Africa, but Truth herself was born in New York. She had never visited the South and did not speak with the heavy dialect associated with southern slaves. The greatest error in the Stowe article was the statement that Truth was dead. She was, in fact, alive and well and living in Battle Creek.

Stowe ended her article by telling how her conversation with the sculptor Story had inspired the Libyan

Sibyl. This statue had just been exhibited at the Great Exhibition in London and had become very popular with the public. Because of this article, people began to identify Truth with the idealized statue.

For the rest of her life, and much to her distaste, Truth was often called the Libyan Sibyl. She reminded people that the facts of her life were found in the *Narrative*, which they could purchase, and not in Stowe's article.

Less than a month after Stowe's article was published, a second article about Truth appeared. It cemented the romantic legend held by the public about Truth. Frances Dana Gage, who had presided over the 1851 Akron Women's Rights Convention, wrote an account of that meeting years later for the *New York Independent* newspaper. Gage's version of that meeting was generally accepted as accurate. In reality, however, there are many questions about her account.

Gage described Sojourner Truth's most famous women's rights speech, in which she used the phrase "Ain't I a Woman" over and over. Truth is quoted as using the powerful, rhythmic repetition of the words to thrill her audience. Strangely these words were not mentioned in accounts published immediately after the convention. Truth did actually give a speech supporting women's rights at the convention, but it was not as long or as powerful as the version that Gage printed twelve years later.

This photo of William Wetmore Story's *Libyan Sibyl* statue was taken in May 1997 at the Museum of American Art at the Smithsonian Institution in Washington, D.C. Story modeled this statue after a description of Sojourner Truth given to him by Harriet Beecher Stowe.

Gage's article contained other questionable claims. The writer asserted that there were objections to letting Truth speak at the meeting. According to Gage, it was only through her efforts as chairperson that Truth was permitted to speak. No other account of the convention mentions this incident. Gage also claimed that Truth said in her speech that she had thirteen children and lost them all to slavery. Truth actually had four children who survived into adulthood. Finally, Gage inaccurately presented Truth's speech in the same exaggerated southern dialect that Stowe had used in the *Atlantic Monthly* article.

Gage's version of Truth was not entirely correct, but it was popular at the time. Together, the Stowe and the Gage articles created a romantic, if inaccurate, version of Sojourner Truth, which became popular during her lifetime, and which still continues today. Truth was shown as a simple, even a primitive, soul who could electrify an audience with a few words of Christian faith. This was an image with which upper-class whites were comfortable. This was the Sojourner Truth who became a national celebrity. Truth herself was never comfortable with this fictionalized image. When she was called the Libyan Sibyl, she said, "I don't want to hear about that old symbol; read me something that is going on now."

9. The Nation Divided

In the 1850s, when Sojourner Truth was first appearing as a forceful figure within the antislavery movement, the conflict between the North and the South over the future of slavery was becoming more and more pronounced.

The Kansas-Nebraska Act of 1854 allowed settlers in the two new territories to choose whether or not slavery would be allowed within their borders. Guerrilla warfare broke out as bands of pro- and anti-slavery supporters flooded in from other states.

In 1857, the Supreme Court ruled that Congress did not have the power to pass laws restricting slavery. This decision in the *Dred Scott* case further convinced northern abolitionists that southerners would try to extend slavery at all costs. They banded together to form the Republican Party, to fight the slavery forces on the political front. Within a few years, the Republicans were powerful enough to challenge the Democrats. By 1860, they even nominated Abraham Lincoln, a young and relatively unknown Illinois country lawyer, for president of the United States.

The elephant was first used to represent the Republican Party in this November 1874 newspaper cartoon by Thomas Nast. Nast chose such a party symbol because he felt that elephants, like Republicans, were determined and clever when calm but unmanageable when alarmed.

During these years, as the divide between the North and the South became wider, Truth continued to hope that the issue could be resolved peacefully. She traveled around the country, urging her audiences to seek a Christian solution.

With the election of Lincoln in 1860, however, the southern states decided no further compromise was possible. War began in April 1861, when Confederate troops attacked Union troops at Fort Sumter in the harbor of Charleston, South Carolina.

Although Truth was more than sixty years old, she continued to work in support of the Union cause. In addition to lecturing, Truth expressed her support in practical ways. For example, she raised money to supply Thanksgiving dinner for the fifteen hundred black troops stationed at Camp Ward in Detroit, Michigan.

Her health was starting to fail. This meant that she was not able to travel as much as she had before, and she could not sell as many copies of the *Narrative* or *cartes-de-visite* to support herself. She and her family experienced financial difficulties, and her friend,

This painting depicts the Confederate attack on Fort Sumter in the harbor of Charleston, South Carolina. The battle at Fort Sumter on April 12–13, 1861, was the opening engagement of the American Civil War.

This first draft of the Emancipation Proclamation was completed by President Abraham Lincoln on July 22, 1862. The Emancipation Proclamation freed slaves in areas still under Confederate control. However, all slaves were not actually freed until 1865, when the Thirteenth Amendment to the U.S. Constitution was approved.

Frances Titus, wrote an appeal on her behalf in the *Anti-Slavery Standard* for contributions. Truth would later use these contributions to buy her Battle Creek barn.

President Lincoln signed the Emancipation Proclamation, which freed slaves in the Confederate states, on January 1, 1863. Although some of her anti-slavery friends were disappointed with Lincoln's gradual pace of abolition, Truth urged patience. "It takes a great while to turn about this great ship of state," she reminded them.

In the spring of 1864, Truth decided to visit Washington, D.C., to "advise the president." As was her habit, she did not share her plan ahead of time. A Battle Creek friend remembered, "When she made her trips she always declared that she had received a call, and none knew when she would be leaving or returning. She would just start suddenly away with a few belongings and would reappear as unexpectedly."

With her fourteen-year-old grandson Sammy Banks, Truth took a train to the nation's capital. On October 29, 1864, Truth and about a dozen others, including two other black women, sat in the White House reception room. In her later description of the meeting with Lincoln, Truth said he showed the same "kindness and consideration to the colored persons as to the whites—if there was any difference, more."

Lincoln was respectful to the former slave and showed her the Bible presented to him by the "colored

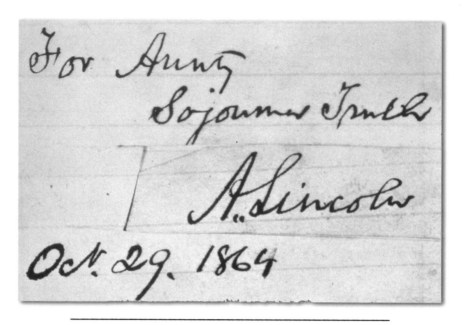

This is the handwriting of President Abraham Lincoln.
When he met with Sojourner Truth in 1864, he signed
her autograph book, which she called her "Book of Life."

people of Baltimore." The president also signed her
"Book of Life," her autograph book, "with the same
hand that signed the death-warrant of slavery." Truth
was deeply moved by her meeting with Lincoln and
vowed to support his reelection effort.

While she was in Washington, D.C., Truth visited
Freedmen's Village, where about sixteen hundred
emancipated slaves were living in terrible poverty.
George Case, the superintendent of the village,
arranged to have Truth live in a cabin in the village and

to use a lecture hall. Truth spent several months working with the former slaves, urging them to develop independence through education. As Case wrote, "She talked to them as a white person could not, for they would have been offended with such plain truths from any other source."

Truth spoke against the attacks on former slaves by slave traders who raided the village to capture blacks and to return them to the Confederate states. Because the slave traders threatened to kill anyone who reported their activities, the freedmen were afraid to protest. Truth was not afraid of reprisal. When bribed policemen threatened to arrest her if she continued to speak out, she replied, "If you put me in the guardhouse, I will make the United States rock like a cradle."

By the end of the year, she was officially employed by the National Freedman's Relief Association to work with the former slaves. In 1870, she was paid a total of $390 for twenty-six months of work. This represented an average income of $15 per month, or less than $4 per week.

Although the slaves in the Confederate states were freed, racism and prejudice were not dead in either the South or the North. While in Washington, D.C., Truth

---

Previous page: This painting of Sojourner Truth's meeting with President Lincoln was made after Truth's death by a Michigan artist named Franklin Courter. Frances Titus paid Courter $100 to do the painting, which he based on Truth's recorded description of the meeting.

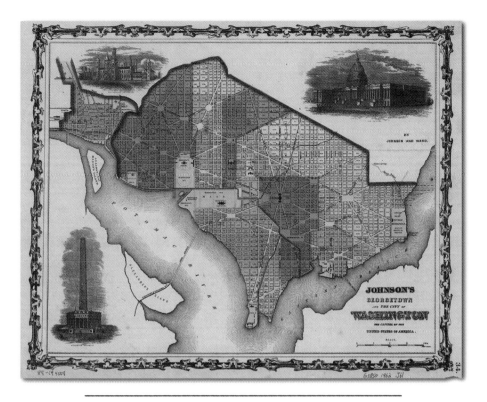

This 1862 map shows the city of Washington, D.C. The Washington Monument can be seen in the lower left corner and the Capitol appears in the top right corner. Sojourner Truth moved to Washington, D.C., in her late sixties, and there she began working with former slaves in the newly created Freedmen's Village.

used the legal system one last time to launch another successful attack on discrimination, this time on public transportation.

Several times Truth had tried to signal a horse-drawn streetcar to stop and to pick her up. The drivers ignored her and drove on, or threw her off the streetcar if she succeeded in boarding. This was in clear violation of a recently passed law, which outlawed racial discrimination on streetcars.

Finally, in September 1865, she and Laura Haviland, a white abolitionist who was working with Truth at the Freedmen's Hospital, climbed aboard a streetcar. The conductor tried to put Truth off, shoving her against the door and bruising her shoulder. When a doctor examined her later and found the shoulder swollen, the women were urged to report the incident to the president of the streetcar company. The conductor was fired and Truth successfully filed charges of assault against him.

Truth was one of several blacks fighting discrimination on the horse-drawn streetcars of Washington, D.C. Her efforts, with the great publicity her name brought to her actions, certainly helped create a climate for change.

At that time in her early seventies, this woman, who had spent her adult life working for equal rights for blacks and women, was close to the end of her career. She was not done yet, though. Establishing a secure home for the recently emancipated slaves became her mission.

10. The Last Crusade

While Truth worked in Freedmen's Village, her concern grew for the long-term future of the freed slaves. These men and women had no education and few marketable skills. She feared that endless poverty, crime, misery, and little else awaited them and their families.

Truth proposed that government land in the West should be set aside for the former slaves. In 1870, she drew up a petition to Congress, stating:

> *Whereas, through the faithful and earnest representations of Sojourner Truth (who has personally investigated the matter), we believe that the freed colored people in and about Washington, dependent upon Government for support, would be greatly benefited and might become useful citizens by being placed in a position to support themselves.*

In the petition, Congress was asked "to set apart for them a portion of public land in the West, and erect buildings thereon for the aged and infirm."

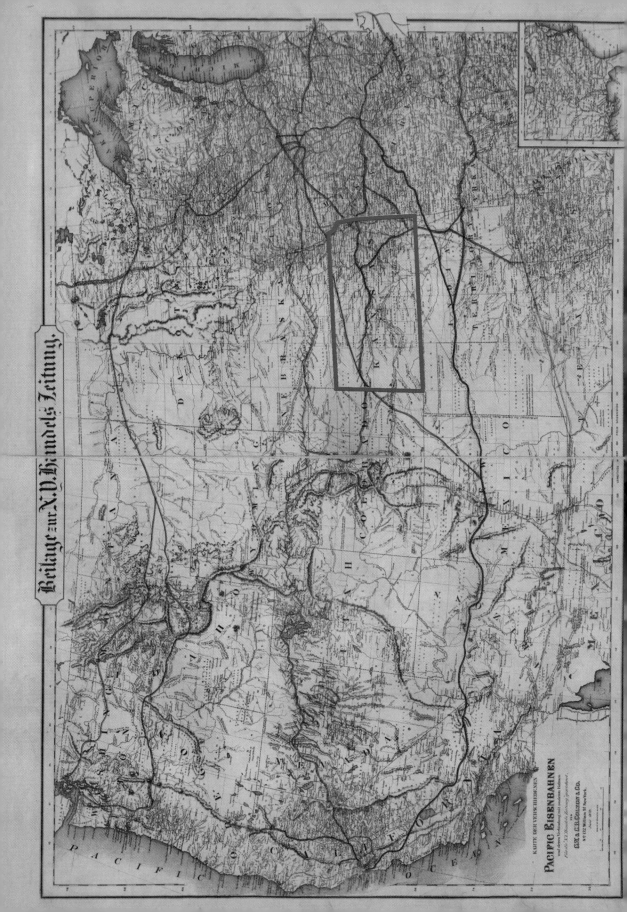

Beilage zur N.Y. Handels Zeitung.

KARTE DER VERSCHIEDENEN

PACIFIC EISENBAHNEN

und deren Verbindung mit anderen Bahnen
für die N.Y. Handels Zeitung gezeichnet

von

GEO. A. C.B. COLTON & CO.
No. 172 William St. New York.
June 1873.

During 1870 and 1871, Truth and her grandson Sammy Banks traveled around New England and the Middle Atlantic states, seeking support for her resettlement project. She went to Kansas for six months, touring possible sites for the farms that she wanted set aside for former slaves.

Throughout this campaign, Truth met with mixed results. Some audiences were large and enthusiastic; others were smaller and unresponsive. At times she seemed to falter and to show her age. At other times, she delivered her message with her accustomed power.

After extended trips and meetings to collect signatures for her petition, Truth returned to Washington, D.C., in the spring of 1874. There is no record that she ever succeeded in actually presenting her petition to Congress before Sammy fell ill and they had to return to Battle Creek.

Twenty-four-year-old Sammy Banks died in February 1875, of complications after an operation. Truth was brokenhearted, as Sammy had been her constant companion on her trips. In addition to her grief, Truth faced poverty. She had no money and was forced to borrow funds to pay for Sammy's medical bills and burial expenses.

Opposite: Kansas is outlined in red to make it stand out in this German map of the United States. In 1879, thousands of former slaves flocked to Kansas from the Deep South, fearing that their newly won rights might be overturned if they remained in the South.

Although it was not the result of Truth's resettlement campaign, in 1879 there was a spontaneous movement of thousands of freedmen out of the Deep South to Kansas. The former slaves feared that the political and the economic gains they had made under Republican control after the end of the Civil War would disappear when the Democrats returned to power in state elections. The freed slaves sought farmland on which they could earn a living for their families.

Truth enthusiastically supported this migration. Despite her fragile health, she returned to Kansas one more time, giving a series of speeches to raise money for the new settlers. Her strength finally gave out and she returned to Battle Creek in January 1880.

This was her final campaign. She stayed near home for her last three years, increasingly limited by recurring ulcers on her leg. Diana and Elizabeth, her two older daughters, lived with her and took care of her.

Truth was ready to join her Lord in Heaven. She told a friend, "I isn't going to die, honey, I'm going home like a shooting star." After a two-month illness, Sojourner Truth died on November 26, 1883. That day she told her family, "The Spirit calls me, I must go." Although she had been telling everyone she was 105 years old, she was actually about eighty-six.

Truth's funeral was held at the Congregational Church in downtown Battle Creek. Reportedly more than one thousand people attended, and several leading

This is a photo of the Congregational and Presbyterian Church in downtown Battle Creek, Michigan. Truth's funeral was held there following her death on November 26, 1883. It was attended by close to one thousand people.

citizens of the town acted as pallbearers. Before Truth died, she had asked that two liberal white ministers, Reed Stuart and Giles Stebbins of Detroit, preach at her funeral. Both men were friends of Truth's from the anti-slavery movement. Truth was buried at Oak Hill Cemetery in Battle Creek. Tributes poured in from around the country, from white and black leaders alike.

Born a slave, Truth became one of the leading figures in the social reform movement in nineteenth-century America. Despite being unable to read or to write and

This is a photo of Sojourner Truth's tombstone. Truth and her family are buried near each other in Oak Hill Cemetery in Battle Creek, Michigan.

having to endure a lifetime of poverty, this remarkable woman gave voice to a generation of blacks and women.

She helped Americans understand the evils of slavery. She had a deep and a personal faith that guided all of her efforts. She became, in her lifetime and beyond, a symbol of the strong black woman who could overcome obstacles and could retain her strength and dignity. No other woman who had been enslaved emerged from the ordeal with the self-confidence to become a powerful public presence.

In choosing her new name after she left slavery, Isabella gave notice of how she would spend the rest of her life. She became a traveling preacher, bringing the truth about social justice to the men and the women of the country. At the end of her life, she could honestly say, "Lord, I have done my duty, and I have told the whole truth and kept nothing back."

Timeline

1797	A slave called Isabella is born in Ulster County, New York, in or close to this year.
1799	Isabella is owned by Charles Hardenbergh.
1806	Isabella is sold to John Neely, with a flock of sheep.
1808	Isabella is sold to Martin Schriver.
1810	Isabella is sold to John Dumont.
1826	Isabella walks away from Dumont to find freedom.
1826–27	Isabella works for the Van Wagenens.
1827	In June, Isabella has a religious vision.
1827–28	Isabella goes to court to get custody of her son, Peter, after learning that he was sold to a slaveholder in Alabama.
1828	Isabella moves to New York City.
1832–34	Isabella lives with the Kingdom of Matthias in New York City and in Sing Sing, New York.

1835   Isabella wins the lawsuit she brought against former residents of the Kingdom of Matthias.

1843   On June 1, Isabella changes her name to Sojourner Truth and starts life as an itinerant preacher.

1843–46   Truth lives in the Northampton Association.

1850   Truth's autobiography, the *Narrative of Sojourner Truth*, is published.

Truth buys a home in Northampton.

Truth gives her first speech on women's rights and begins a career as an anti-slavery and social reform lecturer.

1850–1880 Truth goes on lecture tours of the East, New England, and the Midwest.

1853   Truth visits Harriet Beecher Stowe in Andover, Massachusetts.

1857   Truth buys land and a house in Harmonia, near Battle Creek, Michigan.

1861   The Civil War begins.

1863   On January 1, the Emancipation Proclamation is issued, freeing slaves in the Confederate states.

"Sojourner Truth, the Libyan Sibyl" by Harriet Beecher Stowe is published in the *Atlantic Monthly* magazine.

A newspaper article about Sojourner Truth written by Frances Dana Gage is published.

1864–1867	Truth works at Freedmen's Village in Washington, D.C.
1864	In October, Truth visits President Abraham Lincoln at the White House.
1865	Truth wins a lawsuit against a streetcar conductor in Washington, D.C.
1867	Truth buys a house in Battle Creek, where she lives until her death.
1870	Truth petitions Congress to set aside western land for freed slaves.
1879	Truth begins her final speaking tour, to support migration of freed slaves into Kansas.
1883	On November 26, Truth dies in Battle Creek, Michigan.

Glossary

abolitionists (a-buh-LIH-shun-ists) People who wanted to end slavery in the United States before the Civil War.

activists (AK-tih-vists) People who take vigorous steps in support of or against a controversial issue.

advocates (AD-vuh-kutz) People who speak in favor of someone or something.

American Revolution (uh-MER-uh-ken reh-vuh-LOO-shun) The war that American colonists fought from 1775 to 1783 to win independence from England.

artisan (AR-tih-zen) A person who is skilled in a particular craft.

"Book of Life" (BOOK UV LYF) The scrapbook that Sojourner Truth took with her on her lecture tours. In it she kept autographs and clippings from her speeches.

Civil War (SIH-vul WOR) The war fought between the Northern and Southern states of America from 1861 to 1865.

commune (KAHM-yoon) A small, often rural

community whose members share common interests, work, and income and often own property together.

Confederacy (kun-FEH-duh-reh-see) A group of eleven southern states that declared themselves separate from the United States in 1860–61.

congregation (kong-rih-GAY-shun) The people present at a religious service.

Deep South (DEEP SOWTH) An area of the southeast United States, usually containing the states of Alabama, Georgia, Louisiana, Mississippi, and South Carolina.

denomination (dih-nah-muh-NAY-shun) A religious group.

emancipation (ih-man-sih-PAY-shun) Being set free from slavery.

freedmen (FREED-men) Newly freed blacks in the South after the Civil War.

fugitive (FYOO-juh-tihv) A person who runs away or tries to escape.

illiterate (ih-LIH-tuh-rut) Not able to read or write.

itinerant (eye-TIH-nuh-runt) Traveling from place to place.

juvenile delinquents (JOO-vuh-nyl deh-LING-kwents) Young people whose behavior is beyond their parents' control or even against the law.

medium (MEE-dee-um) Someone who can communicate with the spirits of dead people.

Methodists (METH-uh-dists) Christians who share a particular set of beliefs.

migration (my-GRAY-shun) Moving from one place to another.

Millerites (MIH-lur-yts) The followers of William Miller, who was convinced from studying the Bible that the prophecies pointed to the Second Coming of Jesus Christ in 1843.

minors (MY-nurz) People who are not old enough to be legally responsible for their own affairs.

mutilated (MYOO-tuhl-ayt-ed) Damaged severely.

mythology (mih-THAH-luh-jee) A collection of stories.

New England (NOO ING-lend) A region of the northeast United States.

opponents (uh-POH-nuntz) People who are against other people in a fight, a contest, or a discussion.

premonition (preh-muh-NIH-shun) Anticipation of an event without an obvious reason.

progressive (pruh-GREH-siv) A person in favor of changes or improvements.

Quakers (KWAY-kurz) Members of a Christian religion

founded by George Fox in England around 1650.

radical (RA-dih-kuhl) Favoring extreme changes.

revival meetings (rih-VY-vuhl MEET-ingz) Special services to renew interest in religion.

segregated (SEH-gruh-gayt-ed) To have kept people or things apart from the main group.

slander (SLAN-dur) False statements made to damage a person's reputation.

Spiritualists (SPIHR-ih-choo-wuhl-ists) Members of a religious organization who believe that the spirits of the dead communicate with the living.

Underground Railroad (UN-dur-grownd RAYL-rohd) A loosely organized system for helping runaway slaves escape to safety in the free states before the Civil War. It was run by groups of northerners, which consisted of whites and free blacks.

Union (YOON-yun) The Northern states of the United States of America that fought against the Confederacy in the Civil War.

ventures (VEHN-churz) Undertakings that involve risk or danger.

women's suffrage (WIH-munz SUH-frij) The right for women to vote.

Additional Resources

To learn more about Sojourner Truth, check out these books and Web sites.

Books

Clafin, Edward Beecher. *Sojourner Truth and the Struggle for Freedom,* Henry Steele Commanger's Americans: Profiles of Great Americans for Young People Series. Hauppauge, New York: Barron's Educational Series, 1987.

Krauss, Peter. *Sojourner Truth, Antislavery Activist,* Black Americans of Achievement Series, introductory essay by Coretta Scott King. New York: Chelsea House Publishers, 1988.

McKissack, Frederick and Patricia. *Sojourner Truth, Ain't I a Woman*. New York: Scholastic Press, 1992.

Web Sites

www.huntington.org/vfw/imp/truth.html
www.sojournertruth.org

Bibliography

Mabee, Carleton. *Sojourner Truth, Slave, Prophet, Legend*. New York: New York University Press, 1995.

Painter, Nell Irvin. *Sojourner Truth, A Life, A Symbol*. New York: W. W. Norton Company, 1996.

Truth, Sojourner; Nell I. Painter; Olive Gilbert. *The Narrative of Sojourner Truth: A Bondswoman of Olden Time, with a History of Her Labors and Correspondence Drawn from Her Book of Life*. New York: Penguin Books, 1988.

Index

About the Author

Mary G. Butler is the director of the Research Center of Heritage Battle Creek in Michigan, which houses one of the largest archives of Sojourner Truth material in the country. The Research Center publishes *Heritage Battle Creek*, a journal of local history that has won local, regional, and national awards. A wide variety of curriculum materials, including *Sojourner Truth and the Underground Railroad in Southwestern Michigan*, are available through the Research Center. The center also conducts an extensive Community Legacy oral history program in the Battle Creek area.

Butler graduated from Swarthmore College with a degree in fine arts and received her M.A. in early American culture from Winterthur Museum and the University of Delaware. Before coming to Battle Creek in 1978, she was executive director of the Commission for Historical and Architectural Preservation in Baltimore, Maryland, and conducted educational programming at Territorial Restoration in Little Rock, Arkansas.

Credits

Photo Credits

Cover: Courtesy of the archives of the Historical Society of Battle Creek (both images); pp. 4, 46, 53, 56-57, 58, 59, 65, 69, 70, 72, 73, 74, 88, 89, 97, 98 courtesy of the archives of the Historical Society of Battle Creek; pp.7, 44, 91, 94 Library of Congress Geography and Map Division; pp. 10, 51, 77 © Bettmann/CORBIS; pp. 11, 12, 13, 22, 39 © North Wind; p. 20 Sojourner Truth Institute of Battle Creek; p. 29 Cindy Reiman; pp. 32-33, 40 courtesy of the Phelps Stokes Collection, Miriam and Ira D. Wallach Division of Arts, Prints and Photographs, The New York Public Library, Astor Lenox, and Tilden Foundations; pp. 42, 43, 84 © Culver Pictures; p. 50 © National Portrait Gallery, Smithsonian Institution/Art Resource, NY; p. 52 © CORBIS; p. 62 © Hulton/Archive/Getty Images; p. 78 *The Atlantic Monthly*, April 1863; p. 81 © Richard T. Nowitz/CORBIS; p. 85 Library of Congress, Prints and Photographs Division LC-USZC2-1990; p. 86 courtesy of The Robert Todd Lincoln Family Papers, Manuscript Division.

Editor
Leslie Kaplan

Series Design
Laura Murawski

Layout Design
Corinne Jacob

Photo Researcher
Jeffrey Wendt